A RUM OWD DEW!

Keep a-troshin gal!

Chrsie Hoger

21-05-11

A RUM OWD DEW!

A KOINDLY LOOK AT SUFFOLK

CHARLIE HAYLOCK

With cartoons by Barrie Appleby

COUNTRYSIDE BOOKS
NEWBURY BERKSHIRE

First published 2006
© Charlie Haylock 2006
Reprinted 2006

COUNTRYSIDE BOOKS
3 Catherine Road
Newbury, Berkshire

To view our complete range of books,
please visit us at
www.countrysidebooks.co.uk

ISBN 1 84674 010 X
EAN 978 1 84674 010 7

In Memory of Bill Haylock

Front cover photograph of the Crooked House, Lavenham,
supplied by Clare Calder-Marshall and Alison Englefield

Designed by Peter Davies, Nautilus
Produced through MRM Associates Ltd., Reading
Printed by Woolnough Bookbinding Ltd., Irthlingborough

CONTENTS

Foreword 7

Acknowledgements 10

1 A Brief History of Suffolk 11

2 In a Manner a Speak'n 21

3 A Duzzy Look at Suffolk Trades 33

4 Suffolk Folk Scene .43

5 Suffolk Landmarks .51

6 Grandma's Remedies 58

7 More Ancient Suffolk Surnames 65

8 Suffolk Squit 70

9 The Suffolk Harvest 81

10 A Suffolk Chrissm's 90

   Special Offer 96

Bean 'thrashing' with flail, Weybread, c.1900
(The Museum of East Anglian Life)

FOREWORD

Following the success of my first book *Sloightly on th' Huh*, which was the best selling book in Suffolk in 2004, by a Newmarket furlong, and still going strong today, I was encouraged to write another book about my beloved Suffolk.

A Rum Owd Dew is a natural progression from *Sloightly on th' Huh*, and with the progress of travel, movement of labour, early retirement to the countryside, modern technology, and the like, the old dialects are being lost. Whilst I cannot stem the tide, and I have no intention to try, I do feel passionately about recording the Suffolk dialect in writing, on CD and film, etc., so that it is not lost forever, but will enter the Suffolk archives for our ancestors to look at, listen to and read.

Since completing *Sloightly on th' Huh*, I have appeared several times on BBC Radio Suffolk talking about the history of the Suffolk dialect and Suffolk ways. I have been filmed for, and appeared with friends and associates of mine on Anglia Television's *Country Days*, describing the days of yore in our natural tongue. I have given lectures in Suffolk schools to the sixth form English classes (that's year 11/12 and key stage 4/5 to those gone metric) on the history of the English language and, in particular, the history of the Suffolk dialect.

I have travelled the length and breadth of Suffolk, doing my one-man shows, which portray Suffolk life through 'mardles' and monologues, in village halls and local theatres. I even ventured abroad into Norfolk, Cambridge and Essex, and, believe it or not, I actually crossed the River Thames into Kent and appeared at a venue in Dartford—*Glad t'git back hoom agin*.

I get many requests for after-dinner speaking—ranging from local W.I.s to Masonic functions, from rugby club dinners to local history societies, and from private parties to more public occasions—to spread the word: the Suffolk word, with my 'mardles' and monologues.

These monologues are becoming quite famous. Every time I appear on BBC Radio Suffolk, I am asked to recite one. Afterwards, many listeners ring in and ask where they can get copies. I also get similar regular inquires at all the other venues. You will be pleased to learn, that throughout

A member of Leiston Ladies F.C. in the early 1900s.
(Long Shop Museum)

'iss 'ear book, I've included a *couple a three or so*, of these monologues.

Every language in history that scholars have tried to preserve as a pure, inflexible, unambiguous tongue has eventually died out, Latin and Ancient Greek, for example. We must let languages evolve, and dialects as well, or they will also die. As long as there is a Suffolk, there will always be a Suffolk dialect, albeit vastly different from that of a few years ago. Complaints are made about *furreners* sweeping through the Suffolk countryside and changing the dialect, but if it had not been for so-called *furreners* in the first place—Angles, Saxons, Danes, Normans, etc.— visiting the Suffolk shores, we would not have a Suffolk dialect to save.

What must we do? We must record the sound, write down the grammar, and describe the way of life and how the dialect reflects it. Otherwise, it will be lost forever, and that cannot happen. *A Rum Owd Dew* captures the Suffolk ways and celebrates the unique Suffolk humour. We are lucky to have Barrie Appleby, the legendary, world-famous cartoonist, to illustrate Suffolk wit at its best, throughout the book.

Hopefully, my books will be a Suffolk legacy for future generations to understand and enjoy—and you too.

Charlie Haylock

ACKNOWLEDGEMENTS

I would like to thank the following people, organizations, pubs and clubs, societies, associations and companies, for helping me in my research for this book on Suffolk. Without their input, this book would never have been written.

Mike Acott; Adnams Plc;
Gordon Alecock Snr; Joyce Alecock;
Barrie Appleby; BBC Radio Suffolk;
Derek Baggott; Roger Barnes;
Brandon Heritage Centre;
Clare Calder-Marshall; Peter Carter;
Janet Clarke; Mark Clarke;
The Crooked House Gallery;
Gavin Downes; Edwardstone White
Horse; Alison Englefield;
Girling Collection;
Greene King Brewing & Retailing Ltd;
Bridget Hanley (and all the staff);
Lisa Harris; Bill Haylock;
Kate Hayward; Mollie Hayward;
Barrie Haywood;
Marguerite Haywood; Ed Hume;
Maureen John; Jerv Jordan;

Jordan Engineering; Wendy Kemp;
Long Shop Museum;
Long Shop Project Trust; Julia Mael;
Stephen Mael;
Museum of East Anglian Life;
Network Design and
Implementation Ltd;
The Red Lion, Southwold;
Gerald Rice – Butchers;
The Ryes School; Henry Saltmarsh;
Polly Sambrook; Kathy Scott;
Geoffrey Smith; Stradbroke Library;
Stradbroke Millennium Committee;
Suffolk Records Office;
Mark Taylor; Topic Records Ltd;
Bernard Ulph; Webb Collection;
Westley Club; Eileen Whymark;
Vonny Whymark; Henry Woods.

CHAPTER 1

A BRIEF HISTORY OF SUFFOLK

*A flint knapper at work
(Brandon Heritage Centre)*

S uffolk is steeped in history. Occupation of the area in Neolithic times is evidenced by the flint mines at Brandon and the heathlands around Sutton Hoo and Snape.

A conducted tour at the Brandon Heritage Centre was a treat and the information gleaned was invaluable.

Flint mining and, subsequently, flint knapping, is one of our most ancient industries (not to be confused with our most ancient profession!), extending in Suffolk from Neolithic times to the mid 20th century.

Flints were used as tools, as weapons, as a building material and for making glass. From medieval times to the early 1900s, the Brandon flint mines were famous for their high-quality flints, which were prized for use in firearms such as muskets, flintlocks and pistols, and used by snipers at Trafalgar, Waterloo, and even in the First World War. Indeed, they were so famous that there was a flourishing export trade to the United States of America. It is probably fair to say that Davy Crocket and Daniel Boone would have used Brandon flints.

The heathlands of East Suffolk were once a mixture of woods and scrubland which Neolithic man cleared for grazing. Today, Suffolk Coastal District Council are maintaining certain sites to preserve these ancient heaths.

The Celts

The Celts arrived and spread throughout the whole of present-day England, bringing with them a language that was akin to Old Welsh and Cornish. Suffolk was no exception (although, of course, it wasn't called Suffolk then). The main tribe in East Anglia was the Iceni (pronouned 'Ikeeni'), who gave their name to the village, Iken, and, although they were later driven out, they did leave their mark ... yes! Just take one look at *owd* Doody Wertlingberry from the next village: you know the one ... sings in the choir ... his mother did the milk round ... father worked the land and did a bit of poaching ... sister had an affair with the harness maker ... had to move to 'Ipsidge' ... you know who I mean.

The Romans

In 43 AD Aulus Plautius commanded an invasion, and Britannia was overrun with Romans. They stayed for nearly 400 years. However, the Romans were principally an occupying force and were not settlers. The names that

they found they Latinized: Britannia, Camulodunum and Londinium, for example. They did not create any new names, and not one place-name or one word in the English vocabulary is attributable to the language of the Roman occupation. After the Romans left, however, the Anglo-Saxons who followed gave old Roman forts, settlements and roads' names in their own tongue.

Nevertheless, the Romans were very important in Suffolk. They left behind not only forts, settlements and roads, but also two very important and famous treasure hoards. They are listed in the **British Museum's Top Ten British Treasures.**

Straight in, at No. 5, is the **Hoxne Hoard**, discovered in 1992. This consists of some 14,780 coins, mostly silver, from thirteen different mints representing eight different emperors; 200 pieces of gold jewellery; silver tableware; and a great deal more.

A drawing of the Empress Pepper Pot and coins by Polly Sambrook,
with Barrie Appleby cartoons

A drawing by Polly Sambrook of the silver platter, part of the Mildenhall Treasure

At No. 8 is the **Mildenhall Treasure**, discovered in 1940. The mid 4th-century silver platter measures 2 ft in diameter and weighs 18 lbs. It is among the finest examples of Roman whitesmith craft anywhere in the world. Together with the other 30 or so other items in the hoard, it was truly a great find.

The Angles, Saxons and Danes

In the 5th century AD, the Angles invaded the shores of Britain. They originally settled on the coastline of Suffolk and moved westwards and northwards, taking over a large chunk of land. This was split up into three territories, occupied by the West Angles, the Mid Angles and the East Angles. The latter was then sub-divided into the territories of the 'north folk' and the 'south folk', later to be called Norfolk and Suffolk. Ultimately, the Angles gave their name to the country (England), the region (East Anglia), and the language (English).

Further south it was the Saxons who were raping, pillaging and ravaging the Britons—*noice how d'yer dew*. The land which they took over was split into the territories of the East Saxons, the Middle Saxons, the West Saxons and the South Saxons, eventually becoming known as Essex, Middlesex, Wessex and Sussex. The Saxons invaded the lands of the East Angles, hoping to create a northerly extension of their territory, which by simple deduction

The Sutton Hoo helmet

A RUM OWD DEW!

would have eventually been called Nossex. Thank goodness the Angles stood firm and Suffolk survived, else this book might have been mistaken for a stand for celibacy.

After some toing and froing, a few skirmishes, and a little negotiating, however, the two communities gradually merged, and the foundation of the English language was set in place and the Suffolk dialect was on the scene, albeit completely different from what it is today—or was it? Many Suffolk dialect words are Anglo-Saxon in origin, as described in *Sloightly on th' Huh*. Although the pronunciations have changed, the general sound of the language was created.

The Anglo-Saxon **Sutton Hoo Burial Ship** is No.1 in the **British Museum's Top Ten.** Suffolk now has three entries in the charts. (How can we cope?... Suffolkmania!) This find does illustrate, *howsumever*, how clever, industrious and artistic the Anglo-Saxons were, the Sutton Hoo helmet being a prime example.

During the Anglo-Saxon period, Suffolk was the most densely populated part of England; so, when the people were converted to Christianity, they built more churches there than anywhere else, and it became known as

(By kind permission of Greene King Brewery)

'Holy Suffolk'. The Anglo-Saxon word for 'holy and innocent' was *sælig* (with the *g* pronounced as *y*), which gave rise to dialect *seely*, and eventually *silly*, hence 'Silly Suffolk'. Mind you, I've met a fair few 'owd' Suffolkers who were not so holy and innocent – me included I doubt.

Also during the Anglo-Saxon period, many place-names were becoming established. By-names, too, were in regular use, and many of these, like many of the place-names, were to give rise to surnames in the medieval period. Indeed a large number of English surnames originated in Suffolk, owing to the density of the population.

The Danes invaded northern England, came south, and occupied some of the Anglo-Saxon territory, including Suffolk. It was the Danes who killed King Edmund (later canonized), supposedly at Hoxne, and who the Greene King brewery commemorated with a strong ale. Quite right too! The Danes spoke the same language as the Angles and the Saxons, but they were at the extremes of the language and therefore had completely different dialects. The Danes found it hard to understand either the Angles or the Saxons, let alone the mixture that had formed. During the negotiations (without an interpreter), and the mixing of the tribes, the language inadvertently was streamlined, by using common words and phrases. As a result, female and male genders for chairs, tables, houses, etc. went out the window (thank you Danes!). The grammar became a lot simpler, too, in an effort to understand each other. During the period of Danish rule in Suffolk, villages with Danish names sprang up, such as Barnby and Risby.

The Normans

The Normans invaded in 1066 and stayed. While French was the language of the court and Latin that of the administration and the Church, Old English in its various dialects remained the language of the population at large. But although they conquered, they took on the Angles' language, called it English (*Anglish*) and named the country Angleland, eventually England. This was to distinguish the European Saxons from the Anglo ones. Under the Normans the vocabulary was greatly influenced by French and Latin, with the addition of thousands of new words, although the grammar did not change. There was a very strong presence of Normans in Suffolk, but it kept its Anglo-Saxon roots, and remained an English stronghold. Despite their dominance, there are very few Norman-named villages and towns, and very few Norman-based Suffolk dialect words, other than those words adopted in the English language as a whole. To prove beyond any shadow of doubt that Old English is the foundation of the English language and the Suffolk dialect, take all the words introduced by the Normans out of our vocabulary today and, lo and behold, you will be able to conduct a very intelligent, high powered conversation. However, if it were the other way about, even the most simple of conversations would be impossible. Some of Winston Churchill's speeches were practically devoid of words introduced by the Normans, especially his 'Never Surrender' speech.

The Medieval period

During the Middle Ages, Suffolk was still the most densely populated county, and the richest. The wool trade was centred there, and Sudbury was a centre for the silk trade. Many villages and towns still have their timber-framed buildings from this time, with places like Lavenham and Kersey attracting thousands of visitors each year. It was during this period that Bury St Edmunds and Ipswich started to become predominant: Bury St Edmunds as a market town, with many local industries; and Ipswich as a market town and busy port.

The Suffolk dialect continued to evolve and whilst elsewhere the sound of the language tended to flatten, the Suffolk dialect remained very singsongy, a feature which it continued to keep, and it included the 'double syllable'. Many one-syllable words are elongated by including an additional syllable, for example, clear becomes *cleeyer*, deer – *deeyer*, find – *foy'nd*, four – *forwer*, ride – *roy'd*, seen – *seey'n*, soon – *soow'n*, and many, many *morwer*.

CHAPTER 2

IN A MANNER
A SPEAK'N

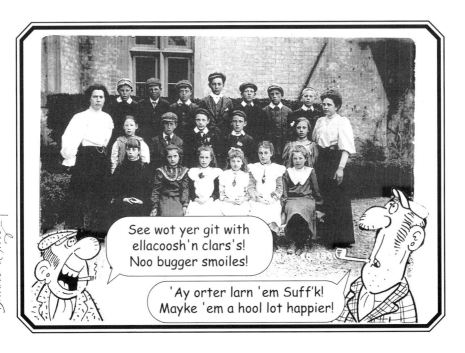

West Row School, c.1900 (Suffolk Records Office, Ipswich)

The Suffolk dialect contains many idiosyncrasies of grammar and expression and, for this reason, is sometimes ridiculed by *furreners*. What is not generally known is that standard English, as we know it today, evolved, basically, in the London, Cambridge and Oxford triangle. Over hundreds of years, so-called scholars have analysed, standardized,

A RUM OWD DEW!

made rules and exceptions for standard English, so that people can understand one another more easily, rather than having to get to grips with loads of dialects. It is fair to say, however, that if standard English had been based on the Suffolk dialect, The Queen might have opened Parliament by saying: 'Moy husb'nd 'n' Oi hed a hully bumpy roide gitt'n heeya s'morn'n. Howsumever, oon't dew a-mardl'n, soo wee'll hatter git along t'gather 'n' oopen up 'iss 'ear Howse.' At home she might say things like, 'Phill'p! Dew yew goo caref'll, bor, with 'eese 'ear corgis, else yew'll trip arse oover hid 'n' hut yourself. Shink wot 'ay'll say in th' paypers.'

The Suffolk dialect is an ancient dialect and is not a *duzzy* way of pronouncing 'proper' English. It came naturally; it was the voice of the *owd* Suffolker. You learnt it from the cradle, not waiting till you got to school and had it forced upon you. It was standard English and its grammar that had to be taught at schools, sometimes reinforced by elocution lessons. Perhaps standard English is a *duzzy* way of speaking Suffolk.

These turns of phrase are common in Suffolk speech:

This here ('iss 'ear) and that there ('at 'air).
(The plural is these here (*'eeze 'ear*) and them there (*'em 'air*)).

'Iss 'ear book's hully good—mayke yer larf.
'Iss 'ear piece a meat's tuff—hatter hully chew.
'At 'air mooter boike goo fairly.
'At 'air clock's allers farst—dew well in Lunn'n.
'Em 'air lowts mayke a nuisance.
'Eeze 'ear hoom-grow'n tayters tayste hully good.

The difference in the two is that, *'iss 'ear* and *'eeze 'ear* are right close or next to, and *'at 'air* and *'em 'air* are farther away. There is not a designated line twixt *'iss 'ear* and *'at 'air*, because it depends on what is being talked about and where.

'At 'air tracter in 'iss 'ear field's goo'n slow.
'At 'air hoss in 'iss 'ear yaard's bit frisky.

22

So it's possible to have *'at 'air*, *'iss 'ear*, but not *'iss 'ear, 'at 'air*; it just would not make sense. Quite simple when it's explained properly.

To confuse the issue, if an *owd Suffolker* is telling a story or yarn, they will refer to the items they are talking about as *'iss 'ear*. This enriches the telling, as listeners can now imagine, whatever is being spoken about, being close by and next to, thereby creating an impelling atmosphere,

e.g. *'Laarst noight Oi wuz on 'iss 'ear boike, noo lights, 'n' 'iss 'ear copper he see mee. Well Oi ...'*

I hope *'eeze 'ear* Suffolk expressions are now fully understood, *'specially boy 'em 'air furreners.*

'On' instead of 'of'

It is common in Suffolk speech to replace the word 'of' with 'on'.

Must'a bin six or seven on 'em.
Heard th' news? Oi wuz towd on ut yesdee.
Rum funny tayste. What's 'iss 'ear cayke mayde on?
Iff 'ay dew 'at agin, hee'll tell on 'em.

In some circumstances the 'of' replaces the 'on'.

Oi allers goo t' chuch of a Sundee.
He goo t' th' pub of a Sat'dee.

I trust this little section is now clear; *Oi oon't keep on a-splayn'n on ut.*

Dew yew (Do you ...)

Dew yew is a very frequent expression amongst *owd Suffolkers*, and is an instruction, not a question, e.g:

Dew yew look arter your pock't munny. Oon't git enny more till Froidee.
Dew he goo caref'll on 'at owd boike, else hee'll fall arse oover hid 'n' hut hisself.

Dew yew keep a throsh'n (or *trosh'n*) was a common well-meaning phrase

Allocation of work, Debenham, c.1910 (P. Carter and H. Woods)

when leaving someone's company. It literally means 'Long may you keep a-threshing', i.e. May you enjoy a long, healthy, active life. The Scottish equivalent is *Lang may yea lum reek* (Long may your chimney smoke).

My father, who went to Snape school in the 1920s, often used to speak amusingly about one of his school teachers. She came up from London and it was her first day in class in Suffolk. Halfway through the morning she said to the class 'Do you have a break now?' All the pupils got up and started walking out of class.

'Where are you going?' she screamed.

'Yew towd uss t'hev a brayke, Miss.'

'No I did not!' she yelled.

The teacher in the next class heard the commotion and had to give the new teacher a lesson on Suffolk grammar. The folk song 'The Candlelight Fisherman' highlights the instruction *'Dew yew'*.

The Candlelight Fisherman (as performed by Bob Roberts)

Moy dad wuz a fisherm'n bowd,
'N' he lived till he grew owd.
'N' he'd oopen th' payne, 'n' pop owt th' flayme,
Jest t' see how th' winds dew bloow.

He'd off'n say t' me,
Afore yew goo t' sea,
Dew yew oopen th' payne, 'n' pop owt th' flayme,
Jest t' see how th' winds dew bloow.

chorus
Jest t' see how th' winds dew bloow
Jest t' see how th' winds dew bloow
Dew yew oopen th' payne 'n' pop owt th' flayme,
Jest t" see how th' winds dew bloow.

When th' north winds roughly bloow,
Oi loie roight snug below,
'N' Oi oopen th' payne 'n" pop owt th" flayme,
Jest t' see how th' winds dew bloow.

When th' wind blow from th' west,
It'll blow hard at th' best,
'N' Oi oopen th' payne 'n' pop owt th' flayme,
Jest t' see how th' winds dew bloow.

chorus

When th' wind blow from th' east,
It's no good t' man nor beast,
So Oi oopen th' payne 'n' pop owt th' flayme,
Jest t' see how th' winds dew bloow.

Continued on page 26

Continued from page 25

When the sowth winds softly bloow,
'Airs not enough few yew t' goo,
So Oi oopen th' payne 'n' pop owt th' flayme,
Jest t' see how th" winds dew bloow.

chorus

Moy woife she say yew know,
Wee'll starve if yew doon't goo,
So Oi oopen the payne 'n' pop owt th' flayme,
Jest t' see how the winds dew bloow.

Now come all yew fisherm'n bowd,
If yew live till yew grow owd,
Dew yew oopen the payne 'n' pop owt th' flayme,
Jest t' see how th' winds dew bloow.

chorus

So, *Dew yew carry on read'n t' gather, 'n' Oi hoop yew're gitt'n th' jist on ut.*

Plurals without the –s

It is common for the –s to be left off Suffolk plurals and, where the plural changes spelling, for the singular to be used as the plural, for example:

Allbra is 'bowt sev'n moile off th' Ay twelve.
Th'ingreediants say three pownd a sugar, not forwer.
Oi hed t' pay two pownd fer a point in 'at 'air hootel.
Moy son Dayv'd he stand six foot tall.
Greedy bugger hev three meal a day.

Having said that, however, Suffolk is famous for its double plurals. Sometimes *docky*, which is a mid-morning snack (so called because the farmer docked the pay for the break), is referred to as *elevenses*. Likewise at 4 o'clock, when it's time for *beavers*, it was sometimes referred to as *fourses*.

> *Moy booy Soim'n gota hully grit owd foot. Tayke soize twelveses.*
> *Moy Aunt counts 'em in twoses 'n' threeses.*

The Old English plural suffix *-en* is present in the English language, in for example, words such as men, women, children, oxen, brethren. In Suffolk, the older generation especially have held on to a few more:

> *At Brand'n bus—'at stop by th' row a cowns'l howsen.*
> *Wee'll hatter stop 'em 'air booys goo'n arter buds' neezen.*
> *Moy cat, she do ketch a hool load a meezen.*

Fourses at Culpho Hall, 1908 (The Museum of East Anglian Life)

A Westley villager, c.1890 (The Westley Club)

Oi say, he say, she say, 'ay say

When *owd Suffolkers* tell a story or a happening where the reporting of a conversation is the crux of the matter, the past tense (said) of the verb 'to say' is seldom used.

> Oi met owd Bill yestdee, 'n' he say t' me 'Hev yew heard?'
> So Oi say, 'Hev Oi heard what?'
> 'N' he say, 'Moy woife Mayble, she say vicar's buggered off with th' cleaner.'

So Oi say, 'What did th' vicar's woife say?'
Well ... Bill say, 'Moy Mayble, she say th' vicar's woife say "Bloody
good ridd'nce"'. "Glad to git rid on 'em," she say.'

Together (t'gather, t'gither, t'gether)

In Suffolk grammar, *t'gather* is a common form of address to people. It does cause some amusement to *'em 'air furreners.*

'Ken we hev yew awl gitt'n on th' bus, one at a toime t'gather.'
'Oi want yew awl t' stand in single foile t'gather.'

If it was time to go out somewhere, whether there was just one other person or several, the instruction would be, 'come along t'gather'. An *owd Suffolker* leaving the pub with one customer left, or a dozen, would say, 'Cherrioo t'gather'.

One of the most amusing stories is when a London school sixth form field trip, went to an East Suffolk Field Centre. At night the girls were in their dormitory and the boys in theirs. But in the morning, when all the boys and girls were sitting down to breakfast, the cook was heard saying to everyone, 'Hoop yew awl slept well t'gather'.

Happen she knew more than what we thought, still, *Haps we move along t' th' next section t'gather.*

Toime (time)

Toime is often used for 'until', 'while' and 'before'.

Oi'll wayte fer a month a Sundees toime acters dew a Suff'k accent.
Oi'll dew moy weed'n, toime yew goo t 'th' shops 'n' back.

Bee'n (being) and oonly (only)

These two terms are often used to introduce a cause or an explanation.

He coon't play t'day, bee'n he wuz injur'd.
She coon't understand th' Suff'k dialect, bee'n she wuz a furrener.
More people bort 'iss 'ear book, bee'n 'at wuz a bess seller.
Oi'd a work't on th' gard'n, oonly 'at wuz too wet.
He'd a gone t' th' match, oonly he hent enny munny.

Suffen (something)

Commonly used in place of 'very' or *hully/hooly*, this appears regularly in Suffolk speech.

Cood a hell, 'at wuz suffen cowd s'morn'n.
'At 'air Lunnener he talk suffen quick, 'n' Oi lissen suffen slow.
Duzzy bugger hed t'say things twoice toime Oi unnerstood.

Shew for showed, etc.

In the English language we have several past tenses ending in –ew, e.g., grew, threw, drew, flew, knew. This is an Old English / Middle English feature, especially with verbs ending in –ow. Since the Middle Ages, most took on a normal past tense with the –ed suffix (bowed, flowed, towed), but Suffolk held on to the Middle English form.

Oi shew 'em how t' do ut.

(It is fair to say that Suffolkers get pulled up more times by outsiders for saying *shew* than for any other word or phrase.

'At suffen snew s'morn'n; snoow wuz three foot deep.
Oi hew th' gaard'n yes'dee 'n' moy back ayke!
He mew th' lawn afore a frorst, duzzy bugger.
Th' owd cock crew at forwer s'morn'n.

Marn't (must not) and dussent (dare not)

These two little words will distinguish an *owd Suffolker* immediately.

Yew marn't goo a chuch in yer work'n clothes.
Oi dussnt be layte fer work.
He dussent cheek th' maarster, else he'll git a clip a th' lug.

Many of these Suffolk expressions and usages are left over from Old or Middle English. It is possible that Suffolk has held on to more Old English/Anglo Saxon words than any other dialect. To show that the Suffolk dialect includes Elizabethan usage, here are a few quotations from Shakespeare:

Another Westley villager, c.1890 (The Westley Club)

'We are such stuff as dreams are made on.' (*The Tempest*)

'You loiter here too long, being you are to take soldiers up.' (*Henry IV*, part II)

'And with another knot five finger tied.' (*Toilus and Cressida*)

So there are all these scholars and learned people learning Shakespearean English at university and at school and having it all explained and experiencing difficulty in understanding it. And there's all these *owd Suffolkers* learning Elizabethan English from the cradle.

What yer cawl suffen straynge.

Finding your way: Some place-names and their pronunciation

Aldeburgh	Awlbra	Kirton	Kerrt'n
Bardwell	Bard'l	Kedington	Kitt'n
Bramford	Brarmf'd	Kesgrave	Kesgr'v
Burgh	Bruff	Lawshall	Lorj'l
Chedburgh	Chedbra	Long Melford	Melf't
Chelmondiston	Chelma/Chelmadist'n	Lowestoft	Lowest'f/Lowerst'f
Debach	Debidge	One House	Wunnerss
Debenham	Deb'n'm	Redgrave	Redgr'v
Felixstowe	F'lixtow/Filixtow	Southwold	So'le
Framlingham	Fraam	Sproughton	Sprawt'n
Grundisburgh	Grunzbra	Stowmarket	Stow
Haverhill	Hayvr'l/'Ayvril	Sudbury	Subbree
Hawkedon	Har'd'n	Walberswick	Wobbleswick
Ipswich	Ipsidge	Wissington	Wist'n

CHAPTER 3

A DUZZY LOOK
AT SUFFOLK
TRADES

I had great fun meeting numerous people and organisations, with wonderful photo collections; I enjoyed sifting through and selecting those which looked, for some reason or other, typically Suffolk. A few modern captions have been added to create additional humour as in the Butchers, the Wheelwrights, and the Bus Drivers. The Fire Service and the Grocer are a bit of fun, whilst the Roadmen has a hidden message. The caption on the Engine Driver picture is not so 'duzzy'. It means that the last train for that day has left; hence the humorous comment.

No matter what humour is being displayed, the underlying theme throughout is how the world has changed. Many trades are disappearing or have already done so. This is alarmingly depicted in the Harness shop picture.

Each photograph shows how perhaps times were hard; a few show that some trades were labour intensive, e.g. the Roadmen and the Butchers. How pre-packaging machines have changed our way of buying food! Underneath the humour, though, is a visual record of how things were. We must never lose sight of our history! Especially Suffolk history!

The Engine Driver (Suffolk Record Office – ref.K/618/1/414/4)

The Butcher (The Webb Collection)

The Wheelwright (The Webb Collection)

The Haywainer (Museum of East Anglian Life - ref.1993.P.3/7)

The Bus Drivers and Conductors (P. Carter & H. Woods)

The Basket Maker (V. & E. Whymark)

The Baker's Boy (P. Carter & H. Woods)

The Tree Surgeon (Museum of East Anglian Life, ref. 77.P.35)

The Harness Shop (P. Carter & H. Woods)

The Fire Service (V. & E. Whymark)

A RUM OWD DEW!

The Grocers (Suffolk Record Office – ref.K681/1/336/35)

The Roadmen (V. & E. Whymark)

The Cleaners (P. Carter & H. Woods)

The Leiston engineers, Richard Garrett & Sons, exported machinery and engines worldwide. This advert is from the firm's late nineteenth-century Spanish catalogue (Long Shop Museum)

CHAPTER 4

SUFFOLK FOLK SCENE

The folk scene in Suffolk still flourishes with many open sessions and folk clubs—so much so, that there are folk activities every night of the week. There are numerous folk dancing clubs and Suffolk step dancing is still surviving. The annual Steve Monk Memorial Trophy is held at The Eel's Foot, Eastbridge during its folk weekend. Young and old participate, but are they as good as Eli Durrant?

One club, in particular, promotes the folk scene extremely well: The Everyman's Folk Club, Benhall, near Saxmundham, which meets at the Benhall and Sternfield Ex-Servicemen's Club. It's a packed house every club night because they follow a successful formula. Members of the audience are invited up to give their renditions, thus promoting the local folk scene, and then the main guest(s), who usually comes from afar (and not just from the British Isles) completes their set. This ensures that many types of folk music and singing are included, and the evening is varied and lively. Most probably this is the best folk club in the East of England, let alone Suffolk, and Steve and Mary Dickinson are to be congratulated for running it so long. They are also influential in organizing 'Suffolk Folk', which not only produces a quarterly magazine but also helps to finance visits to Suffolk schools by certain folk acts, so that children and young people can hear, in song, the history and heritage of Suffolk and places further afield.

One such Suffolk folk song which depicts our past, is entitled 'A Merry Song on the Duke's Late Glorious Success over the Dutch in Southwold Bay', commonly known as 'The Battle of Sole Bay'. This battle was so important that the famous Sole Bay Brewery, Adnams & Co., commemorated the battle with a fine ale called 'Broadside'.

Eli Durrant, with Fred Pearce and 'Wicketts' Richardson, performing at the Ship in Blaxhall in 1953 (Topic Records Ltd)

The Battle of Sole Bay

One day as I was sitting still
Upon the side of Dunwich hill,
  And looking on the ocean,
By chance I saw De Ruyter's fleet
With royal James's squadron meet;
In sooth it was a noble treat
  To see that brave commotion.

I cannot stay to name the names
Of all the ships that fought with James,
  Their number or their tonnage;
But this I say, the noble host
Right gallantly did take his post,
And covered all the hollow coast
  From Walderswyck to Dunwich.

The French who should have joined the Duke,
Full far a-stern did lag and look,
  Although their hulls were lighter;
But nobly faced the Duke of York,
Though some may wink and some may talk;
Right stoutly did his vessel stalk
  To buffet with De Ruyter.

Well might you hear their guns, I guess,
From Sizewall-gap to Easton-ness,
  The show was rare and sightly;
They battered without let or stay,
Until the evening of that day;
'Twas then the Dutchmen ran away—
  The Duke had beat them tightly.

Of all the battles gained at sea,
This was the rarest victory
  Since Philip's grand Armada;

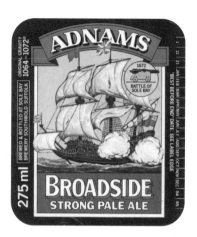

(Derek Baggott, The Red Lion, Southwold)

I will not name the rebel Blake,
He fought for *Horson* Cromwell's sake,
And yet was forced three days to take
    To quell the Dutch bravado.

So now we've seen them take to flight
This way and that, where'er they might,
    To windward or to leeward;
Here's to King Charles and here's to James,
And here's to all the captains' names;
And here's to all the Suffolk dames;
    And here's the house of Stuart.
Anon

Another folk song which describes a more murky past is the 'Murder of Maria Marten' (1824), known as the notorious 'Red Barn Murder'. This rendition gives William Corder's side of the story. He was the fiendish murderer, who was publicly hanged at Bury St Edmunds, before an 'audience' of some 6,000 people. After the customary death mask was made, he was skinned and his hide was tanned, later to be used for binding the book, which was published as the official account of the dastardly deed and the trial that followed.

Fred Pearce playing the melodeon, c.1939 (Topic Records Ltd)

Maria's surname was Martin but the London reporters did not fully comprehend the Suffolk dialect, and, hearing her name pronounced *Mart'n*, they *writ* down *Marten*, which it has stayed ever since.

The Murder of Maria Marten

Come all you thoughtless young men, a warning take by me,
And think of my unhappy fate, to be hanged upon a tree;
My name is William Corder, to you I do declare,
I courted Maria Marten, most beautiful and fair.
I promised I would marry her upon a certain day,
Instead of that I was resolved to take her life away;
I went into her father's house the 18th day of May,
O come, my dear Maria, and let us fix the day.

If you'll meet me at the Red Barn, as sure as I have life,
I will take you to Ipswich town, and there make you my wife;
I straight went home and fetched my gun, my pickaxe and my spade,
I went into the Red Barn and there I dug her grave:
With heart so light she thought no harm to meet me she did go.
He [sic] murdered her all in the barn, and laid her body low;
The horrid deed that he had done she lay bleeding in her gore,
Her bleeding and mangled body he threw on the Red Barn floor.

Now all things being silent she could not take no rest,
She appeared in her mother's house, who sucked her at her breast,
For many a long month or more, her mind being sorely oppressed,
Neither night nor day, she could not take no rest;
Her mother's night being so disturbed, she dream't three nights o'er,
Her daughter she lay murdered, upon the Red Barn floor;
She sent her father to the barn, where in the ground he thrust,
And there he found his daughter, mingled with the dust.

My trial is hard, I could not stand, most woeful was the sight,
When her jawbone was brought to prove, which pierc'd me to the heart;
His aged mother standing by, likewise his loving wife,
And with her grief her hair she tore, she scarcely could keep life.

Adieu, adieu, my loving friends, my glass is almost run,
On Monday next will be my last, when I am to be hung.

So you young men that do pass by, with pity look on me,
For murdering Maria Marten, I was hanged upon a tree.
Anon

Mardles and monologues are also common on the Suffolk folk scene. This next verse, a monologue penned by yours truly, is a humorous protest to town and city drivers, with some advice on how they should drive along the Suffolk lanes.

Driving in The Countryside
(or There are Two Types of Tud)

chorus

'Iss is fer droivers from th' city 'n' tow'n,
Jest a little advoice, on whoy t' slow dow'n,
Whoilst droiv'n along th' country lay'ne,
'N' how t' be courteous, 'n' use yer bray'ne.

'Iss will help yew, tew rea'd th' rood ahead,
Tew avoid th' gestures 'n' th'' swear'n,
'N' git wayves 'n' "thankyers" instead,
'N' end up a droiver more care'n.

Out for a drive (V. & E. Whymark)

'Air are tew toypes a tud, loy'n on the lay'ne,
'At 'at's lumpy, 'n' 'at 'at's play'ne.
'At 'at's lumpy, not long dropp'd,
'At 'at's play'ne, a long toime plopp'd.

chorus

'At 'at's play'ne , beware th' ray'ne,
'At's loike waarter on grease, 'n' becomes a pay'ne,
Hit 'at wrong, 'n' yew're slipp'n 'n' sloid'n,
In th' hedge, or ditch, yew'll be hoid'n.

'At 'at's lumpy, please tayke care,
Or hard t' th' roight, yew'll hev to' veer,
Fer if tuds a still steam'n, s'not far from its rear,
Th' beast's row'nd th' corner. PLEASE BEWARE!!

chorus

If tuds are lumpy 'n' small—sheep ahead,
If 'ay're lumpy 'n' medium—goots ahead,
If 'ay're lumpy, large 'n' flakey—hoss's ahead,
If 'ay're large flat 'n' row'nd—cattle ahead.

At 'iss moom'nt a conjectcha,
Oi knoow what happ'ns Oi betcha.
Oi knoow what th' townie will say,
'What if 'air hent enny tuds? Ay!!'

Oi s'pose th' question is fair.
BUT 'airs oonly one arnser Oi ken afford yer.
Yew gotta TAYKE EXTRA CARE!!

. . . .

Cos 'at's when 'ay're cumm'n t'wards yer!

SUFFOLK LANDMARKS

The Scallop Shell on Aldeburgh beach (Wendy Kemp)

Here's a humorous look at some of Suffolk's landmarks: famous ones, not so famous, picturesque ones and perhaps not, controversial and some obvious ones. The bubble captions in each, depict Suffolk humour; in a few, there is a prime example of straightforward logic, which also makes an observation, hitherto not seen. The Scallop Shell at Aldeburgh was certainly controversial, and the caption depicts what

some locals think. My own view is that it is a fitting monument to Sir Benjamin, but perhaps should have been on the beach in the centre of Aldeburgh, not stuck up the north end. Maggie Hambling, the sculptor, has been known to say that if it's not controversial it's not worth doing. On that theory, it was well worth doing.

The straight-faced logic is certainly seen with the Maltings caption and Willy Lott's Cottage. The House in the Clouds is a bit of fun, as is Orford Castle. Grandma's statue was included because Giles should stand alongside Gainsborough and Constable, as a famous Suffolk artist, although a different genre.

The comment on the Sizewell Nuclear Power Station, (yes, it is a landmark – *a biggen at 'at*) is once again straight-faced logic, with an observation that is shared by many locals. The Mildenhall air base has a similar message.

Obviously not all the landmarks have been included, but in time, in future editions, they will all be covered.

Snape Maltings (Wendy Kemp)

The House in the Clouds, Thorpeness

Woodbridge Tide Mill (Wendy Kemp)

Willy Lott's Cottage, Flatford (Suffolk Records Office – ref. K/681/1/140/50

Grandma's Statue in the centre of Ipswich, commemorating the cartoonist Giles (Wendy Kemp)

Sizewell Nuclear Power Station (Julia Mael)

The Ancient House, Ipswich (Joyce Alecock)

Mildenhall Airbase

Orford Castle (Suffolk Records Office –
Ref. K681/1/347/41)

CHAPTER 6

GRANDMA'S REMEDIES
(From Top t' Toe)

An afternoon visit to my Auntie Kathy, with my mother, was most enlightening, especially when they started talking about illnesses and complaints. These two mature ladies (I *dussent* call them old or ancient) described the old-fashioned remedies that were used when they were young. A visit to the doctor's was too costly at 3d a visit; furthermore, if you did go to the doctor's, it was for something serious. The logic is, therefore, if you don't go to the doctor's, it's not serious. Below are some of the remedies.

Backache

1. Rub the patient's back with horse oil—while he/she lies, face down. Place a large sheet of brown paper on the well-oiled back—and then apply a fairly hot smoothing iron.
2. Strap on thermogene wool, to be kept on all day.

Cataracts

Close the eye and on the lid rub the morning dew off a cowpat (making sure it's only the dew!).

Chest Cold

Rub camphorated oil on the chest and leave.

Common Cold

1. Sip a full bowl of onion gruel.
2. Place feet in a mustard bath.
3. Place three drops of eucalyptus on a handkerchief to sniff regularly.

Congestion of the Lung

Soak a cloth in boiling water, stretch it out and cover it with linseeds; fold it into a pad and place it on the chest until the pad goes cold; repeat the whole process.
   Alternatively, make a bread poultice and place it on the chest.

Constipation

Take a teaspoon of syrup of figs or a teaspoon of liquid paraffin or a dose of castor oil.
   (Note: Take only one remedy at a time, not all three, else you will be looking up the cure for the runs.)

Corns

Use a very sharp cut-throat razor, and slice off the corn gradually
   (Note: Do not worry about septicaemia as it was unheard of in those days.)

Cystitis

Put nettle leaves (preferably young ones) into cold water and bring to the boil, strain, and drink as a tea.

Earache

Place a hot onion, cut in half, behind the ear.

Eczema

Grate finely the root of a dock, put it into water and bring to the boil.

Drain off liquid and mix the dock with pure butcher's lard. Rub a generous amount of the ointment on the rash.

Headache

Soak a rag in vinegar and tie it round the head.

Heartburn

Chew on a piece of ordinary chalk, found in the ground and thoroughly washed.

Indigestion

Mix thoroughly together 3d worth each of bismuth, limewater and peppermint oil and swallow.

Nose bleed

Place a cold key or penny on the back of the neck.

Piles

Get an old leather boot; set fire to it and let it smoulder. Put it into an old metal bucket. Sit down on a bucket, exposing the delicate area to the smouldering. Wait till the smouldering stops. (Think I'd rather have smoked bacon!)

Rash (or hoomer)

Place marigold leaves into boiling water and allow to boil for a few minutes. Strain and drink as a tea.

Runs (the)

Grind up a piece of chalk, and eat it with a lump of cheese.

Sore ribs

Rub on a good layer of goose fat, cover with brown paper and strap on. Keep on all day and repeat daily until the soreness goes.

Alternatively, as above, but use a stockinette tube instead of strapping.

Sore throat or dry cough (tizzick)

One teaspoonful of lemon juice, one teaspoonful of honey, and one teaspoonful of vinegar. Mix thoroughly and take.

Stomach ache

Drink a tot of gin in hot water.

(Note: If the pain is severe, try two tots. Caution: If taken too frequently over a short period of time, concerns for the stomach ache will disappear, but those for drunk and disorderly will come to the fore.)

Toothache

Rub oil of cloves onto the gums near the affected area, or, alternatively, place a clove on the affected tooth and chew.

Wasp or mossie stings

Place a wet blue bag on the affected area.

Postscript

If I had to try some of these remedies, I think I would want to get better fast, just to avoid the remedy! Howsumever, at the time of writing, my mother is 86, (her father lived till he was 90), my aunt is 77 (her father lived till he was 92), and my father lived till he was 88; so perhaps these remedies did work!

It is of a medical nature which inspired me to write this next monologue. In the village where I used to live, we never went to the doctor's, we went up the pub, either on a Tuesday or Thursday morning. The doctor would come to the pub and set up his equipment. The saloon bar was the waiting room and the tap room his surgery. All that separated the two was a piece of temporary marine-ply and a curtain, and if you listened very carefully one side, you could hear what was on the go, on the other side. We learnt a lot, but I have changed the names to protect the innocent.

Th' Doctor's Village Wait'n Room

Yew're off t' th' doctor's, feel'n mangey 'n' ill.
Yew're after a poult'ss, a powder even a pill.
Th' wait'n room's full, everyone there.
How are yew? A' yew okay?
A' yew awl roight? Yer hear'm say.
What a' yew a-doo'n heeya?

Young Dizzy Whymonger's three week overdew,
Th' place 'n' how – she carn't remember who!
Th' day, th' toime – she carn't remember when,

'At could be a variety a men.
Darkie Deac'ns reck'ns its him – huh – he wish.
Ay reck'n it's the man who bring row'nd th' fish.

'Awl alone 'n' sat in th' corner,
Doubled up – wuz Smelly Warner.
'Ay let'm alone – 'ay coont get neeya
Th'air wuz thick – 'at brought a teeya
Non-stop flatulence wuz th' problem at hand –
But Smelly coont smell – so he dint understand!

Snipper Dow'nes wuz 'air – one degree under,
Spent awl noight on th' choina gazunda.
He troid awl noight, but awl in vain –
He grunt'd 'n' grunt'd, again 'n' again.
He stroived 'n' strained – but ought could he parss
So he got tew serpositrees................
................'n' a hospital parss!!!

How are yew? A' yew okay?
A' yew awl roight? Yer hear'm say.

Uncle Charlie had swallerd his glass oye
We didn't know how 'n' we dint ask whoy.
'At caused 'm grief – in a bit of a stew!
Three days gone, 'n' 'at hent pars'd threw!
He dropp'd his trousers 'n' oover he bent –
Th' doctor knelt dow'n 'n' under he lent.
'Well! I can't see a thing – That's a bit of a do'
'At's a bloody rumm'n doctor!...Oi ken see yew!'
'Yer left oye's oop'n 'n' yer squint with th' roight!'
Th' doctor fell backards in surproise 'n' froight!
His fust case a hoindsoight!! Hent sin one afore,
'N' he'd bin a doctor thutty year a more.

Make'n a fuss 'n' harnsen about, Owd Fossy Corder
Suffered fer years with hysterical disorder.

She wuz last one in, 'n' wanted t' be fust!
Else 'at's tew late 'n' she be buried in th' dust!
She say, she's dropsy, shingles, a wart 'n' hoyait'ss hernia!
Ringworms, rick'ts, baldn'ss 'n' hoyperchondria
Hiccoffs, the gowt 'n' chick'n pox!
She say Th' Grim Reaper is com'n t' measure th' box
Tubal Alecock calmly stated – ' Good damn 'n' blast!'
With 'at little lot – yew hent got long t' larst!
Hev yew troyed alternatives: holistic, akipuncture 'n'
aromathreppy
Reflexology, crystalisation, 'n', hommyoperthy?'
'Huh! Oi ont wanner ketch enny a 'em – certainly not!
Oi've anuff on me plate, with 'iss little lot!!

Yew're off t' th' doctor's, feeling mangey 'n' ill,
Yew're after a poult'ss, a powder, even a pill.
Th' wait'n room's full – everone's 'air.

How are yew? A' yew okay?
A' yew awl roight? No Oi 'm bluddy not Oi say!
Oi'm leav'n in a hurry – ont be back aggin!
Oi've caught more in heeya, 'an when Oi come in!

Cheerio!!

CHAPTER 7

MORE ANCIENT SUFFOLK SURNAMES

A large number of English surnames were first recorded in Suffolk, owing to the fact that the county was once so densely populated. Many Anglo-Saxon names refer to either the elf or the wolf. The elf was seen as noble and the wolf as being powerful and strong.

Here are just a few names first recorded in Suffolk prior to 1200 and still in existence today.

Aldrich/-ridge	personal name: 'elf' or 'noble ruler'
Aylward, Elwood	personal name: 'elf or noble guard'
Burrage/-idge	personal name: 'strong fort'
Cates/Kates	a nickname: 'happy, jolly'
Clay(s)	'clay', hence possibly occupational for a claypit worker
Earwoker/ Erricker	occupational: swineheard
Flint(er)	from either a nickname for someone hard as flint or perhaps occupational for a flint knapper
Garnish	a nickname for someone with a moustache
Goodall/Goodale	'good ale': nickname for a brewer/innkeeper
Levitt	loved one or Norman for wolf cub.
Platten	'metal plate', hence occupational for a plate maker
Randolph	personal name: 'wolf shield'
Shanks	nickname for long legged
Talbot	a bandit or robber
Town/-e/-es/-s	by, or on a farmstead (not an Ipswich Town supporter)
Underwood	living in or below a wood

Walwyn	personal name: wolf friend
Widger	personal name: elf spear
Woolard/	personal name: wolf guard
Woolward	
Woolmer	personal name: wolf leader
Woolston	personal name: wolf stone

*Bill Haylock pictured in 1907, on his 18th birthday
(Joyce Alecock, née Haylock)*

Haylock is derived from an old local Angle chieftain, Haegul (pron. Hay'l), The son of that chieftain would have been called Haegluc. It was not until 1188 when the name was first recorded officially. This was in Bury St Edmunds, and written as Heiloc.

Hayward was an Angle occupational name, *hegeweard* (pronounced 'Hayward') meaning `hedge or fence guard', whose job was to keep livestock away from crops. The name, written *Heiuward* and *Haiuuard* is recorded in the late 11th century in Suffolk (Bury St Edmunds). The Suffolk dialect word for hedge is *hay* and the job of layering and interweaving live hedges is called *haywarding*.

The Hayward family at a tennis party at Farnham Hall, c.1912 (Mollie Hayward)

A RUM OWD DEW!

Bones as a surname was first recorded in 1327 in Suffolk and the above is an example of the Suffolk double syllable, and the confusion it sometimes creates.

Ulph is from an Old Scandinavian personal name meaning 'wolf' (Old Norse *Úlfr*), which is recorded in Domesday Book (1086), in Suffolk as *Ulfus*. As a surname it is recorded in Bury St Edmunds in 1125 as *Wlf*.

Charles Ulph, c1900, Ipswich (Bernard Ulph)

CHAPTER 8

SUFFOLK SQUIT

This chapter gives examples of Suffolk *hoomer*, including Suffolk *squit*. The latter can best be described as nonsensical and illogical logic. Norfolk and Suffolk are very close on the funny side of things and great banter is prevalent between the two. Not so Suffolk and Essex, and definitely not Suffolk and Cambridgeshire.

Suffolk and Norfolk are the East Angles, forming the region known as East Anglia. I can recall three surveys conducted by the media on regional humour, with London, Liverpool and Newcastle vying for first place each time. East Anglia was bottom of each survey/poll conducted. Part of our sense of fun is that our humour is not understood by *furreners*. Each one of the polls endorsed that. Only we knew it was funny.

The pub scene captions are typical Suffolk humour, and endorse our sense of fun.

The Fisherman and the Yachtsman

After a hard day's work fishing, a Southwold fisherman went into his local for a well earned pint of Adnam's Brown Ale (or a couple a three, more like). He was approached by a 'weekender', a yachtsman up from London.

'Good evening,' he said.
'Eevn'n,' the fisherman responded.
'Have you been out today?' asked the weekender.
'Yeah,' was the short reply.
'So have I. Blowing a northerly, you know.'
'Is 'at a fact?' was the fisherman's response.
'Yes indeed. You have to be extra careful when the wind lies in that direction,' the weekender informed the fisherman.
'Is 'at a fact?'

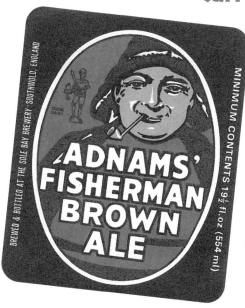

*(Derek Baggott,
The Red Lion,
Southwold)*

'Yes,' said the weekender, and then proceeded to tell the fisherman, who came from a long line of fishing folk (father, grandfather, great grandfather, generations of 'em) the different approaches and techniques of getting into Southwold harbour, depending on which way the wind lay—northerly, sou'westerly, easterly, nor'nor'east; if the wind is backing this way or veering that way—on and on he went, every direction imaginable. He paused.

Suddenly the fisherman stepped in, 'At's a bloody rumm'n, bor. Ev'rytoime Oi goo t' sea, th' wind allers bloow in th' sayme derection, 'n' 'at's a fact!'

'And what direction is that then?' asked the weekender with a sarcastic tone.

'T'wards me!,' was the emphatic answer, with a dead-pan face.

With that the fisherman left the disbelieving, wide-open-mouthed yachtsman standing at the bar. As the fisherman went through the door, he turned and sang 'See how th' winds dew bloow', and then disappeared. He had sung a chorus line from a very famous Suffolk fishing song, which would have been handed down from father to son (see Chapter 2).

The Retirement Dew

A farmhand had worked on the farm for 50 years, having left school at 14 and gone straight into work on the farm. Being too young for one war

and too old for the next—his might even have been a reserved occupation—
he was never called up. After 50 years' continuous service for the one
farm and three generations of the farmer's family, he was approaching 65
years of age, and retirement loomed. The village hall was booked with a
band and a buffet. All his family and friends (seemingly the whole village)
were there, and the farmer's family, too.

Things were hotting up, with dancing and drinking. Suddenly, the
music stopped. It was time for the presentation. A space is made. The *owd*
farmer, the 'Major', makes a speech about loyalty and hard work, and
presents the farmhand with his retirement present.

The farmhand slowly opens (never do anything quick in Suffolk) the
present. The farmhand looks aghast.

'Whoy hev yew bort me wunner these?'

'It's your retirement present.'

'Oi know. Whoy hev yew bort me wunner these?'

'It's a watch.'

'Oi know it's a bloody watch. Whoy?'

'It's a gold watch.'

'Oi know it's a bloody gowd watch. Whoy?'

'It's your retirement present.'

'Oi know. Oi've work't fer yew close on 50 year a more. Oi wuz never
layte once!'

Everyone smiled except the farmhand and the Major. The Major, who
was taken aback, not sure which way to take it, tried to make conversation.

'No, no, no—never late once. But you never wore a watch.'

'At's roight.'

'Being on time in the morning is easy: you had a clock at home. But, no
matter where you were on the farm, at the end of the day you knocked
off dead on time—no watch, no clock—how did you do it?'

'Eezy. On th' other soide a th' far field is th' grammar school loine. At
foive fifteen ev'ry day, th' grammar school train goo past onnuts way to
town. Soo Oi left fifteen minnuts aforehand. Eezy!'

The farmhand walked away and asked his wife for a dance. They both
had a glint in their eye, and they danced and drank the night away. He
was late next morning for church, however—the first time he had ever been
late in his life... and the first time he had ever owned a watch.

The Train Journey

In my research, I interviewed an old farmer in his late eighties/early nineties – he wasn't quite sure which. He said that he had lived in his village since the day he was born, never anywhere else. 'Booy! Oi've oonly bin t' Lunn'n once in moy loife!' he say.

'Doon't want t'goo agin!' he added.

'Went t'see a soliciter – bowt thutty, forty year agoo!'

'Oi got on th' tray'ne t' come hoom, sat 'air, awl t'moyself'.

He described how there weren't any inter-city trains; it was practically all stops from Liverpool Street Station to Ipswich – about a two-hour journey. There were no corridors along the train, just a door one side, a door the other and bench seats, the width of the carriage, facing each other – a picture of Southwold above one seat, and a picture of Aldeburgh above the other.

'Tray'ne start'd off, 'n' awl of a sudd'n, a fella in a pin stroipe suit, booler hat, brolly 'n' a brief case, starts racen th' tray'ne – duzzy fool'. Th' door floy oopen 'n' 'iss 'ear fella falls in – slams th' door 'n' sits oppers't'.

74

The farmer then relived the following conversation:

'Eevn'n!'

'Oh! Good evening. Where are you going?'

'Ipsidge.'

'So am I; it takes about two hours, you know',

'Is 'at a fact'.

'Why don't we play a game of I-Spy – help pass the time?'.

'No! Oi just wamt t'goo t' sleep 'n' wake up in Ipsidge.'

'Why don't we play Twenty Questions – help pass the time?'

'No! 'N' wee'd need more 'an twenty questions twixt heaya 'n' Ipsidge!'

'We must do something – let's have a general knowledge quiz.'

The farmer apparently told him what he could do with his general knowledge quiz, somewhere where the sun don't shine.

'Let's make it interesting – I ask you a question, if you get it right, I give you ten pounds, but if you get it wrong, you give me ten pounds, and vice versa'.

'How menny toimes dew Oi need t' tell yew?'

'Okay – okay – okay, if you get it right, I give you a hundred pounds,

and if you get it wrong, you give me ten pounds. Any questions you ask me, I get it wrong, I give you one hundred pounds. I get it right, I get ten pounds'.

'Mmmm ... Awl roight ... yew goo fust.'

'What were the closing prices of Rowntrees on the stock market this afternoon?'

Well the farmer didn't know the answer and he handed over ten pounds.

'Your go, your go.'

'Don't hurry me, Oi'm Suffolk ... What goos up hill with forwer legs, 'n' comes dow'n hill with three?'

'Pardon?'

'What goos up hill with forwer legs, 'n' comes dow'n hill with three?'

Well, the city man didn't know the answer, he handed over a hundred pounds to the farmer.

'Well ... what does go up hill with four legs and down with three?'

The farmer waited a while ... thought ... and gave the city man ten pounds back. He also reminded the city man, that it was the farmer's go again.

Never judge a book by the cover, eh?

A RUM OWD DEW!

CHAPTER 9

THE SUFFOLK HARVEST
A Family Affair

U p to the late 1800s, and even the early 1900s, harvest time was a family affair. The men, led by 'the Lord a th' Harv'st' used scythes (*soyes*) to cut the corn. Other men folk and women folk would tie up the sheaves and stand them in small self-standing groups (*shock 'em*). Children were let out of school for the harvest, and it was called 'harvest holiday', though not what we would call a holiday these days. Harvest took precedence over school. The youngsters would help where they could,

Harvest workers, c.1890 (The Girling Collection)

Harvesting with a sail-cutter c.1900 (The Suffolk Record Office, Ipswich – ref K/681/2/23/10)

especially culling the rabbits when they tried to make a break for it, as the area of standing corn got smaller and smaller.

So important was the harvest, that if it failed, the village folk would know hard times and hunger throughout the winter. Therefore it was essential that everyone got stuck in. If anyone was late for work, they were fined and they were also fined if they started fighting amongst themselves in their efforts to get work. Yes – times were hard.

Led by 'the Lord', a group of up to a dozen men would work in unison scything the corn, all the time moving together in a steady rhythm. When 'the Lord' stopped to sharpen (*rub*) his scythe, they all stopped. The art was to *rub* the front and the back of the blade. It was important to keep a sharp scythe at all times, else *at 'oont cut, 'n' 'at'll pull ut up b' th' roots.*

Meanwhile, the group following would be making a tie, with a few stalks of corn, twisted in the middle, to bundle up the sheaves. These were then stacked in shocks. The constant bending caused the workers to suffer indigestion and heartburn; so a common remedy was for people to put a piece of chalk in their mouth, and suck on it all day. Three acres cut, sheaved and shocked was a good day's work. To shield themselves from the sun, the women folk would wear large bonnets to keep their faces as white as the driven snow: *Oont want yer fayce scortch't up loike 'ay dew t'day.*

Then, in Victorian times, the scythe gradually started to disappear— mechanization had begun! The first machine to make its mark was the clipper reaper. This caused pandemonium. Village folk thought it would cause unemployment so they would get up very early in the morning and throw metal bars, sticks and poles into the cornfield to sabotage the new machine when it was set to work. They really did think this was the devil himself, the Grim Reaper!

Another new invention was the sail cutter. This was a dastardly machine, requiring balance and timing. It consisted of rotating blades and although it cut the number of scythe reapers down, the vast following army was still required. The string binder followed and this was a *marster* machine. When first used, hundreds of folk would make the journey to whichever farm it was at and just stand, watch, and marvel.

Whichever methods of reaping and binding were used, the job that followed after the sheaves had been shocked was to load them onto the

A spectacle to behold: a string binder in action, 1905 (The Museum of East Anglian Life – ref A2084.1)

wagons, using a pitchfork. This was a steady job and not one to be rushed, *else yew'll bugger yerself up fer th' arternun*. Again, everyone lent a hand. The wagons had to be steered into the stack yard (*stack 'ud*) just so, exactly on the right spot, so that the sheaves could be unloaded and built into a stack.

Stacks were built in any of three shapes: round, boat-shaped, or gable-ended. They were then thatched to keep them dry.

The whole process—from cutting the corn to thatching the stack—was done with the utmost urgency, to ensure dry corn and a dry stack. If the wheat or barley got wet, then people would starve in the winter—harsh but true.

Any rabbits that had been caught during the harvest were auctioned off, which was a bonus for the workers. And then, of course, came gleaning, when the workers were allowed back into the fields to gather what had been left behind on the ground. Everyone in the family gleaned, collecting as much as they could. An 18-stone *coomb* of wheat would yield about

(V. & E. Whymark)

A family takes a break for 'noonings' c.1890
(The Girling Collection)

15 stones of flour, which in turn would make about 120 loaves of bread and thus help to keep the family alive through the hard winter. The gleaning was strictly controlled. Once the harvest had been gathered, a shock was left behind in the field to act as a 'policeman'. A bell would ring and the 'policeman' was taken away as a signal that the workers could start gleaning. They had approximately twelve hours to collect their 'free issue', and then the bell was sounded again. Anyone found gleaning outside this allotted time would be in serious trouble and could even be 'exported' to Australia for the crime.

The harvest finished with a *horkey* or harvest supper. This would consist of something grand, like broad beans and boiled pork, washed down with a beer and mangle wine mixture. People also drank strong old beer that had been brewed in the March specifically for the *horkey*. It was a time to celebrate, and it resulted in a few sore heads the next morning.

During the winter months, the sheaves were taken from the stacks to the barn. And as the stacks got lower and lower, then more and more

Threshing at Blythburgh, 1910, showing a No 4 Compound Garrett steam motor tractor driving a Garrett finishing thresher and elevator (Long Shop Museum)

mice and rats would run out. Children were given the job of killing them and were paid according to how many they caught. Long trousers with *lijahs* (leg straps worn below the knee) to avoid the vermin running up your legs were the order of the day.

In the barn the corn was threshed with a flail *(a stick 'n' a harf)*. This would be done by a number of men, all in time, like a team of bell-ringers, e.g. 1 - 2 - 3 - 4 - 5 - 6 — 1 - 2 - 3 - 4 - 5 – 6, etc. Mind you that would mess them up fairly if the foreman shouted *Goo Canterbree Choimes!* or *Goo Granser Doubles!* After the corn was threshed, the team would then use their large winnowing shovels and toss the corn into the air. The doors of the barn were open on both sides, causing a stiff through draught to separate the wheat from the chaff. It was then bagged, and stored to be used as and when required.

The mechanization of agriculture continued, with the introduction of the steam engine and the threshing machine. Suffolk manufacturing companies were at the forefront of this revolution, with companies like Garrett, Ransomes, Jeffries, Smythes, and Catchpole, some of which would become world famous.

So many different machines were coming onto the scene, it was very hard to keep track; more often than not, very difficult to follow 'the instructions', with all the new technological words that had never been heard of before.

My grandfather used to explain, with great amusement, how sometimes they got into a *roight buggers muddle,* with all the *technacalarties.* It's from those amusing stories, I penned 'Th'New Fandangled Thingamabob', and ridiculed the new vocabulary which sounded to the untrained ear, like a load of *gobbledegook.*

Th' New Fandangled Thingamabob

'What's at Oi see, cumm'n on t' the farm?'
    'Don't worry chaps – that'll do you no harm!'
'Oi tell yew what – 'At's a rum owd job!'
    'Don't worry – that's my new fandangled thingamabob!'.

Chorus

'At bit 'air, look a rum owd tool!'
    'Anyone can work it – even a fool!'
    That'll take another ten minutes of the job!
    This new fandangled thingamabob'

'Now this splicer oojit flipper band,
You hold very tightly in your left hand.
You twist it around, a third of a jip,
And the ignition thingy will continually flip'.

'Now you turn the reamer bindy wheely thing,
Now the engine will really sing.
The spindle flapper gubbins – push with your right foot,
And this will stop the build up and clogging of soot.'

Chorus

'You go up and down, with the split cable handle,
Till the furnace glows, like a roman candle.
The thresher special jumper pin, kicks into gear,
And the flapper helm plate, you have to steer.'

'You control the latest spring back throttle,
But keep your right eye on the fuel gauge bottle,
Your left eye on the binder lever marked 'C',
That you have to control with your left knee.'

Chorus

'The V-plate G-clamp goes to and fro,
And the turnscrew cutter blocker goes like so.
The spindle feeder cappit flue,
Is governed by, the left hand tappit screw.'

'The heater whatsit detector arm,
Will crankle up the fire alarm.
So the super thingy cooling flow,
Needs to operate – at ten below.'

Chorus

'Howd yew hard!', Say the gathered throng.
'What happ'ns if the bugger goos wrong?'
  'Like we have always done on the land!
  We'll do it by horse and we'll do it by hand!'

'What will Oi do, with th' half hour Oi 've gleaned?'
  'Easy! You get a brush, and you keep it cleaned!
  That in itself will take an hour and a bit.
  So you will have to fill in – an overtime chit!'

They looked at the monster,
And started to curse!
And made up a rhyme,
And put it to verse!

'Now 'iss bit heeya, look a rum owd tool!
No-one would boy ut ...oonly a fool!
Th' salesm'n certainly knew who t'rob,
When sell'n our marster, 'at new-fandangled-thingamabob!'

In the winter months the traction engine and threshing tackle would turn up on the farm. The whole set-up had to be exactly level, else it wouldn't run for long. Once it was level, the stacks would be gradually loaded onto the threshing machine, driven by the steam traction engine, with dust, dirt and chaff flying everywhere—*th' wind wuz allers in th' wrong direction fer someone.* It was all washed away with a good drop of ale later that day, including a pint or two of Adnams Best I doubt.

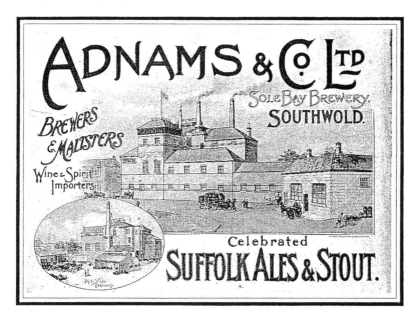

(D. Baggott, the Red Lion, Southwold)

CHAPTER 10

A SUFFOLK CHRISSM'S

(Mrs Kathy Scott)

I n the days of yore, up to the mid 20th century, many Suffolk folk would fatten up a bird for Christmas. They would feed it on good scraps and *'barley mung'.* However, the bird became too fat on most occasions to put in the kitchen range to cook. So what happened? The village bakery would come to the rescue. My Uncle Reg and Auntie Rosie kept such a bakery, in the heart of Suffolk. On Christmas Eve, the local folk would go along with their trussed-up goose or chicken or turkey, and handover their intended meals.

My Uncle and Aunt would be up at the crack of dawn, if not before, and place the birds into the baker's oven, at varying times, dependent on size, so they would all be cooked at roughly the same stage. The villagers would turn up, late morning, take their Christmas bird away, properly wrapped. By the time they got home, it was just right to carve.

This was a common practice and is an example of how villagers helped one another, especially at Christmas time.

I appeared on 'The Mark Murphy 05 Christmas Show' on BBC Radio Suffolk. Together we had a 'Suffolk Christmas Squit' morning. As usual, I was requested to recite a monologue, one I had *writ* especially for the occasion, depicting how Christmas has changed, and perhaps how it's lost its true meaning. Afterwards, as normal, many listeners rang in requesting a copy. You need not wait any longer:

Chrissm's

'At's Chrissm's morn,
Kids are up – afore 'at's dawn.

Th' stock'ns are oopen – Soo full a glee,
An orange fer yew – An apple fer me.
A penny chew – a chocky bar tew
Brazils 'n' waln'ts – jest a couple or three.

At's Chrissm's morn,
Mum is up – afore 'at's dawn

A grit owd turkey – she haff t'cook,
Twenty minnuts a pow'nd – plus twenty – 'At'll be plenty,

Soo Deliah say – in her little book.
Stuffed galore with sossidge, sage, onion 'n' toime –
Chessn'ts tew – But – 'at didn't roime!

'At's Chrissm's morn,
Everone's up – Dicisions are torn

Brekf'ss fust – 'en th' presents we'll oopen
Th' young'ns showt – OOPEN 'EM NOW!
NO! screams Dad! – Huh – He ent coop'n
Th' noise levels roise!
Everyear th' sayme – noo serproise.
Dad gits his way – 'n' brekf'ss is set
Th' kids gulp ut dow'n – Oi don't hink 'at wuz ett!
Dad ent finished – but 'ay'll still hatter wayte –
Fer Granny 'n' Grandad – 'n' Owd Auntie Kayte!
The kids are now – in a hellava stayte!

'At's Chrissm's morn,
Th' kids awl shrik'n – Awl forlorn.

At last – At last – Everone's heeya
Howd yew hard – Grandad's oopn'n a bottle a beeya!
At last – At last – Dad sits by th' tree.
Who wants t'help? Me! – Me! – ME!!!
One at a toime, th' presents are sort
.....Look what Grandma's bought –
'n' Grandad oop'ns his bottle a port
Dad's got hankies – a tie 'n' some socks –
Grandma's drink'n scotch on the rocks
Mum's got underwear – awl skimpy 'n' frilly,
OH NO! Grandma 'n' Grandad are now gett'n silly.
The kids get games, some sweets 'n' toys
Dolls fer th' girls – Meccano fer th' boys.
A grit owd spaceship, in a hooly big box.
Auntie hev oop'n'd her favour't chox
Paper – Paper! – PAPER galore!

Strewn awl oover – th' liv'n room floor.

'At's Chrissm's Day – we're goo'n up a pub –
Leave owd Mum, t' cook th' grub.

Yew ken hardly move, up th' Dog 'n' Pheas'nt
Everone wear'n – a Chrissm's pres'nt.
Tordy is wear'n his silk cravat –
Ruffles is wear'n his new wooly hat –
Pullovers, ties are all in view –
'N' Dad – with his pair a socks tew.
'Air's poor Owd Thatch, 'n' twin brother Bert
Both are wear'n – an Hawaiian shirt –
'N' a pair a shorts – with awl 'em zippers –
Yes! Yew've guess'd – Both are wear'n, their new bedroom slippers!
Th' pub is full – annual commotion –
A peculiar aroma; - a blend of ...?
Dozens of ...? After-shave lotion!

'At's Chrissm's Day – We're still up th' pub –
Mum's still at hoom – cook'n th' grub,

Everone know exackly what t'dew –
Drink a fair few 'n' back boy tew.
Th' fust points are dow'nd
Dad is boy'n – anuther row'nd!
Grandad is goo'n at a fair owd rate –
He says 'at's fower – But we know 'at's ayte!
'At's toime t'goo – 'At's nearly tew,
Dow'n th' lane – 'n' at th' double
Don't be late – else we're in trouble.

'At's Chrissm's Day – 'N' th' big turkey roost,
Let's awl see who can eat th' moost.

'Air's turkey breast 'n' turkey wing
Oh No! Grandad's tipsy 'n' wants t'sing.

A RUM OWD DEW!

Roost pertaters 'n' parsn'ps tew,
Grandad's staggered off t' th' lew
Mash'd pertaters – along with th' swede
Sprowts 'n' carr'ts – Cor – one hellaver feed.
Stuff'n with sossidge, sage, onion 'n' toime,
Chessn'ts tew – 'n' 'at still don't roime
Gravy juice, 'n' cranbree sauce
Ah Yes! 'N' baked suet pudd'n a corse!
Dad poors th' woine – full t' th' top,
Grandad tew – but he doont know when t' stop
We pull th' crackers, with a hellaver crack
Everone wear'n – a funny hat.
Th' jooks are corny – but we don't moind,
It's th' little trink'ts we carn't foind!
Dad stands up 'n' proposes a toost –
Then everone tucks in – t' th' turkey roost.
Everone eats – fit t' bust!
BUT – When yew think yew've had yer fill –
Th' Chrissm's pudd'n – is a must
Covered in brandy 'n' set aloight
With the lights turned off – make a lovely soight.
Vanilla cust'd 'n' clotted cream,
Th' brandy butter is just a dream.

'At's Chrissm's Day – At's Chrissm's Day –
Th' Queen at three – shall hev her say.

Grandad's oopn'n anuther beeya
Th' telly's turn'd on – 'n' awl must heeya –
She wish's uss well – her feel'ns a deep –
It's easy t' tell – But Grandad's asleep.
Th' rest a th' day is mayhem 'n' stress!
Wash'n up, clear'n up – putt'n away!
Watch'n th' film – play'n a game
Ever Chrissm's – jest th' same!
Grandad's sleep'n, 'n' some hev a rest –
Th' kids – th' kids – soo full a zest!!

One by one – 'ay awl woind dow'n
'En awl of a sudd'n – not a sow'nd
Dad wakes up 'n' soo does Mum –
Chrissm's day is nearly done.
'Ay pick up th' kids 'n' carry 'em t' bed.
Shush – shush – not a wud is said
Th' adults t'gather – downstairs once more
Everone awake – 'n' Grandad is start'n t' pour,
A few more brandies, a port 'n' a beeya –
Everone happy 'n' full a good cheeya
Chrissm's day has come 'n' gorn –
Did ennyone remember? ...
'Iss wuz th' day ... Jesus was born?

*Stockman and carter, George Goldsmith, c.1890
(The Westley Club)*